This book is dedicated to my loving grandmother, Yado Amna, my greatest inspiration my mother, and my forever supporting father. And finally, to you! The reader of my first published book! I hope you find in between these covers something unique and special, something new and different, something you won't find in any other book.

Aisha Alawadhi

FRAGMENTS OF REMINISCENCE

AUSTIN MACAULEY PUBLISHERS™
LONDON • CAMBRIDGE • NEW YORK • SHARJAH

ISBN – 9789948770053 – (Paperback)
ISBN – 9789948770046 – (E-Book)

Application Number: MC-10-01-1016389
Age Classification: E

First Published 2024
AUSTIN MACAULEY PUBLISHERS FZE
Sharjah Publishing City
P.O Box [519201]
Sharjah, UAE
www.austinmacauley.ae
+971 655 95 202

The long concealed emotions are revealed,

Into a book of poems,

I wrote them when I was only thirteen,

And now everyone knows them,

How I feel and how sensitive I am,

Towards the things around me,

And all of that you know,

But be careful not to tell the story,

Now I'm asking you readers a favor,

For me not to mence,

Please do not use,

My book to tease or threaten,

Cause I forever will haunt you,

Even when you've forgotten.

Death

There's not a relief as the relief of death,
It shall come once in one's life,
It's touchy and sad yet happy,
It shall end the pain of one's life,
It leaves not a breath in one's heart,
It drains all the blood in one's veins,
No more pain you shall have,
No more tears of one's eyes,
Yet tears that slide down other's cheeks,
Are tears of love to whom rests in peace,
"Rest in peace," they say,
No more tears nor ears will hear,
The voice of one whom rested in peace.

Mother

Every time the moon is full,
We remember someone's face,
Someone who sang us songs,
To go to bed and stop the play,
One who carried us nine months,
And gave birth to ones,
This person whom smiled and cheered,
Whenever her child achieved,
Whether it was a one or a ten,
She'd smile brightly once again,
I'd like to call her whenever I,
Achieve something great oh-my,
She'd laugh and smile again and again,
For me to feel proud and giggle,
Thank you, Mother, I love you,
More than every ink drop!

The Greatest Man

Nothing like late drives with you,
Funny stories, things I never knew,
Many lessons, lectures too,
Life is hard, but happy with you,
You were the first man that held me,
Tiny I was, but I looked like you,
Your hands so big, so much you give,
Had my back forever, it's time I have yours,
Protected me like a diamond, always loved me,
Your words saved me, when I was empty,
If I were a man, I'd want to be like you,
You are the greatest man I'll ever know.

The Pain of Survival

Not all scars are shown,
Not all wounds heal,
You can't always see
The pain somebody feels,
Life is short,
Appreciate ones around you,
Before happy moments,
Turn into tearful memories,
Not everyone that started with you,
Will end with you,
You'll lose loved ones,
And be blessed with others,
However losing one,
Can blind you enough,
To not see others,
Missing someone,
Can cause you deafening,
Always be aware of good ones surrounding you,
And never forget the ones that left you,
'Cause ones who leave us,
Don't really leave us,
They're always going to be there,

'Cause no matter where they go,
They'll never leave our sides,
Nor leave us alone,
They'll be found deep in your heart,
Behind an unbreakable rock,
Never hurt someone,
'Cause you'll get it back,
Do not conceal your emotions,
Nor show them to anyone,
'Cause honest emotions
Can be used as a weapon against you.

Grandmother

Under the crying sky,
She sat down,
Ignoring the rage of thunderstorms,
Or listing to singing birds,
During summer or winter,
Spring and fall,
She read a holy book,
Unlike any other,
She prayed and prayed,
With every prayer,
And every letter she read,
She shed tears,
A purer heart there shall no be,
A kinder human will never walk on this earth,
A loving caring person there will never be,
"My grandma,
My grandma," I say,
May God bless you with every step,
May God protect you,
May God give you the happiness you deserve.

Words

Words are powerful,
Words are strong,
Words can hurt,
Words can't heal,
Words can haunt,
Words can break,
Words can burn,
Words can be felt,

Three things always remember,
What you show,
You will see,
What you say,
You will hear,
What you give,
You will get,

You will never need,
What you desire,
You will never desire,
What you need.

Life

Life is unfair,
Life is hard,
What you ask for,
You'll never get,
What you need,
You pay for with your sweat,
What people show,
Is never true,
People hide,
People seek,
Sometimes you're strong,
Others you're weak,
Never forget,
That at the end,
Blood drains from veins.

Drops in the Ocean

For whom my words are just drops in the ocean,
May God bless you wherever you are,
No matter how dark my nights were,
You were always a blessing from God,
A moon that shown in the darkest of the nights,
To say the sun will rise again,
A figure that spread love and warmth,
A far better than a human,
An angel whom gentleness and pure heart,
Loved the world and all the people,
Black, white and of all colors and tones,
Prayed for in every prayer,
Thought of in every step,
Loved with all her heart.

Mother II

To the one whom my words,
Are worthless toward,
My sun, my moon,
My all-in-one package,
My first yet greatest teacher,
My closest and best friend,
My first responder,
My happiness,
My sense of humor,
My joy and all my laughter,
My most precious diamond,
I love you more than anyone's ever gonna know,
You're one which words can't cherish,
You're one which I can't describe,
For you're the most pulchritudinous human,
Not only outside but inside too.

Know

I don't want your help,
Nor do I want your advice,
I only want some words,
With no lies,

Some words worth hearing,
In other cases reading,
Words worth my time,
Not hurting nor blaming.

Words I can listen to,
Words I can understand,
Words I can respect,
Words I can respond to.

Failure an Old Friend

I say it all the time,
But I can't even make it rhyme,
I need an exit door,
Into another floor,
I can't believe I'm nearly there,
Until I know I lost, unfair,
I tried my hardest to accomplish,
Yet failure's my companion,
I'm not stopping yet,
I can still feel it,
The feeling of never giving up,
Even if you and failure are tied with coughs,
Keys and locks were made for purposes,
And I'm not stopping yet,
I'm greeting failure as an old friend,
A one which I'll meet again,
Not today, nor tomorrow,
But at the neverlands.

Spring

I cling to hope as a human,
Wanting no less than success,
Knowing cherries blossom,
And flowers of all colors,
Singing birds in spring,
Listening to my poems,
I'll write and sing,
Read and repeat,
Every day is a new adventure,
One brave,
The other led by curiosity,
But fun rules at the end,
All ladies are beauties,
We love them filling duties,
And everyone has one,
Something they're the best at,
Even if it was something small,
It's greater than you'll ever know,
Once you try it though!

You

Thunder roared,
While the sky mourned,
Lighting breaks,
But no one cares,
Days are running,
Yet no one's listing,
I'm lost in a valley,
I can't even think of a good phrase,
I need nothing,
Literally no one but you,
For my day to bloom.

Days

Day after day,
Week after week.
Month after month,
Years after years,
Are all days,
All different,
All unique,
None similar,
None alike,
New experiences,
New adventures,
Non repeated,
Non dates in margins are alike,
All come and go,
In 24 hours it's another day!

God

It shone brightly every night,
After the sun left the sky,
Peculiar and bizarre,
Yet lovely to the eye,
Created by God Almighty,
Who rules the seven skies,
The one whom I pray for,
Day and night,
In summer and winter,
Fall and autumn,
Whom I cry to,
And thank in regards,
The one who I say my wishes to,
And *Inshallh* he'll grant.

Rashid

Every time he looks up at me,
With his innocent eyes,
Either filled with tears,
Or begged for my phone,
I can't say no, for his purity,
His request can't be declined,
Every time he holds my hands,
His warm tiny fingers,
Are ones which I find comfort in,
For they're the love itself,
And when he asks me,
With curiosity or concern,
I can't but answer him,
For he's the one I can't return.

Dreams

It long haunted me,
For I can't count,
Countless is better in the context,
Yes for countless times,
It sang into my ears,
And straight to my mind,
I thought of it for hours,
If not days, my, my,
Fonts and colors,
Word after word,
Letter by letter,
And here I am,
If you're reading this,
Know I've achieved,
One of my biggest dreams.

Curiosity

If it wasn't for curiosity,
Humans today would've been cavemen,
If it wasn't for mice's curiosity,
Cats wouldn't have chased them,
If it wasn't for the cat's curiosity,
She wouldn't have died,
Curiosity is the thrust, the engine,
Of a car called life,
Without curiosity,
There is no chance of survival,
For curiosity is the brush of an artist,
For curiosity is the hammer of a carpenter,
For curiosity is the pen of an author.

Dubai

You call it Dubai,
I call it home,
Where I belong,
My heart, my soul,
My precious ones,
Where I go,
Without an invite,
Where I can laugh,
Where the sunshine is bright,
Whenever in doubt,
Just come and visit,
Knock on the doors,
Of my favorite place.
From the heart of Dubai I write,
Under the moonlight.

Aunt R

She stuns,
She's fun,
She's one in a million,
She my beautiful auntie, how much I love her,
Beautiful on the out and inside too,
Smells like flowers, sounds mellifluous,
Her voice melodious,
Loving and astonishing,
Kind and crafty,
Board games she shares,
Daring yet caring,
We love her in perpetuity,
In August she's born,
She deserves a throne.

Tears

Warm, no hot tears sliding down my cheeks,
Tears of pain, of sadness, of hate,
Hard to disguise, even when I'm alone,
No sense of relief, no happiness, no cure,
For pain taught me, and is my greatest teacher,
For it taught me that life is unfair,
Everything, I gave everything for ones,
Yet I got nothing, nothing in return,
Breakdowns, mental breakdowns every day,
Too much going on inside my brain,
Growing bigger, resenting more with every tear,
This is not the cup of tea I wanted,
Yet it is the best I can possibly get,
Nothing can heal me, no one can understand,
My feelings now are far beyond humans' knowledge,
Only he understands, for he is the Almighty,
I read his holy book,
And all the pain is washed away.

Letting Go

Farewells are happy,
Try keeping them tear free,
Never rage when it's farewell,
It might be,
The last time you see one,
It might be,
The last of your conversations,
It might be,
Your last time together,
It might be,
The last time you see them,
Always say,
Goodbye when it's farewell,
'Cause it's either good,
Or maybe the last.

The Doctor of the Soul

Kind and loving,
Loves all and everyone,
Sweet and beautiful,
Bewitching, astonishing,
In parties she greeted,
Mornings she waved,
Farewells she smiled,
A huge wide one,
Magical and appealing,
She never raged,
Nor yelled,
Kind words only she said,
She's my Auntie Ayesha,
The doctor of the souls.

The Flow

I call it the flow,
For it's unstoppable,
Words follow words,
I can't stop them,
I write them,
I read them,
I love them,
I keep them,
I pour my feelings into them,
Loving me more with each word,
For they contain,
My sadness, my pain,
My happiness,
And all my feelings.

Sore Sight

And she swayed under
The whistling wind
She stood gracefully
In pride
Oh such beauty
And yet one glance
She was given
Five seconds of length
How long it took
Years and years of pain
Of the sun and running water
To become such a sight
A sight for the sore eyes
And yet no one
Showed a hint of appreciation
No one admired the beauty
I apologize, dear flower,
Please forgive us humans
For we are not worthy of your beauty.

Thoughts of the Wind

Oh you don't know,
How much I wish I was a flower,
Or a bird,
For they alone,
Know true peace and happiness,
For they understand,
The meaning of freedom,
For I never tasted that thing called happiness,
I heard it was good,
But who cares,
Something you can't possibly ever buy,
Nor find like treasure boxes,
It doesn't have a map,
Nor a location,
It's made,
Only you can make you happy,
Always remember that,
Only you can make you happy!
The beginning is tough,
Yet it's all worth it,
Try once or twice,
If failed try again.

Bleed

When happy they're there,
When ill they leave,
When trusted they backstab,
When needed they betray,
Never get too close to people,
Who'll break you,
When you're at your most vulnerable position,
Happiness isn't given by people,
It comes from God,
In a world that doesn't know mercy,
You're either a victim pleading,
Or a criminal gambling,
A silent knight,
Or a burning match,
You either demand change,
Or make change,
Be the change,
Or witness the change,
You either give it your best,
Or never taste a teaspoon of rest,
We asked and got rejected,
So now we demand,

We were abandoned and unheard,
So now we'll make sure we get what we want,
You either give us what we need,
Or loose the lead!

Lecture

Sometimes we cut people out,
We know it's for the best,
But we also feel the tragic pain,
You think you'll get over it one day,
But you don't know if that day is coming.

Sometimes we wish they were here,
But on second thoughts you remember,
That they don't want you anymore.

Sometimes we feel like texting them,
Or sending them a relatable meme,
But you remember that you don't text anymore.

Sometimes you watch over your snaps,
From one year ago,
And you see this person smiling and giggling,
You looked happy together,
You thought the friendship was evermore,
But you remember that they replaced you.

Sometimes you wish something you did,

Was something that you never did,
You blame yourself for something you didn't do,
Until you realize they don't need you.

You trusted people,
Who were fine with betraying you,
You gave them all you had,
But they couldn't care less,
You needed them but they were never around,
Your vulnerability and fragility satisfied them,
Your soreness and agony pleased them,
Your burning tears elated them,
Your fueled anger thrilled them,
They're monsters behind a cheap, ersatz mask.

Barista

She felt so much pain,
Her feelings all long void away,
Lost all the happiness she ever had,
Nothing can heal her anymore,
Physically and mentally broken,
All her scars are open,
Giving anything for the cure,
She's exposed and insecure,
Vulnerable and fragile,
She long lost her bewitching smile.

You can tell by the taste of her tea,
Changed as if not a single spoon of will,
Was added to the bag of the tea,
The smell was different,
The taste was insufficient,
What happens to such a pure heart you ask,
Someone whom favorite thing,
Was making tea and selling it to people,
I favored her tea,
Not only for the taste or the smell,
But mostly for the love poured,

Into each single bag,
What can affect such a strong lady,
To lose her will and her pureness,
May she once again,
Find the will that was treasured,
Deep inside her pure, white heart.

Until Next Time Dear One

It hit me hard how little time,
We spent together, worth more than a dime,
Never knew you'd leave this early,
Never in my wildest dreams,
Did I think you'd leave,
Without a leaving slip,
Without a single warning,
Or a good goodbye,
I don my hat to you,
Yet you'll never don back,
I'm totally missing you,
And I want you to know,
That you're kind lovely figure,
That left my sight,
Will never leave my heart,
Nor will it move aside,
Your bright, gracious smile,
And your lovely days of holy Quran,
Will remain in mind,
May we meet again,
Next year, dear one.

Hamdan bin Rashid

(May he rest in peace)

To the person who believed and invested in youth talents.

And he left,
A kind figure, a pure, white soul,
One whose care,
Reached those in the darkest of hells,
You of the white hands they call,
Hands which carried everyone around,
A big heart you had,
The gifted you educated,
The orphans you raised,
The homeless you placed,
In a happy place,
The hungry you feed,
The sick you remedied,
The unable you treated,
May you of the selfless, altruistic soul,
May you rest in peace,
And may Heaven be your home place.

Take Notes

Talk less, work more,
Don't fight with a single roar,
Break fake illusions, build dream sets.

Never open your door to someone who'll knock once and
leave,
'Cause people who knock once,
Won't last long,
Open your doors to people,
Who will knock until their knuckles bleed,
Because people who wait for you,
Will remain with you.

When asked answer,
When rejected leave,
Never stay with those,
Who your worth don't see,
If mad, don't shout,
When annoyed, don't ease,
Fight back for your honor,
Fight back for your believes!

Piece by Piece

And again I'm punished,
Again I'm blamed for a crime I didn't commit,
Again you curse, push and leave,
Again you lock a door behind you,
Again I'm alone in the dark,
With ripped, old moth-bitten curtains,
Ones which I can't fix,
Again I'm left behind, duets and squads unite,
Again I'm alone,
Crying, haunted by your deaf tones,
Again I'm left broken,
I'm healing my self piece by piece,
May peace rest with me,
'Cause one day my soul will levitate,
Hopefully to heaven in the 7th sky.

The Final Chapter

My heart's shades,
Sealing blades,
Black and gray,
Clear my way,
Looking good,
Carving wood,
Brushing floors,
Opening doors.

Ending books,
Changing looks,
New chapters,
Wing flatters,
You have to choose,
Or you'll lose,
One or two,
Feeling blue.

On my way,
Sing hooray,
My happy soul,
Achieving my goals.